Catherine Murphy

New Work

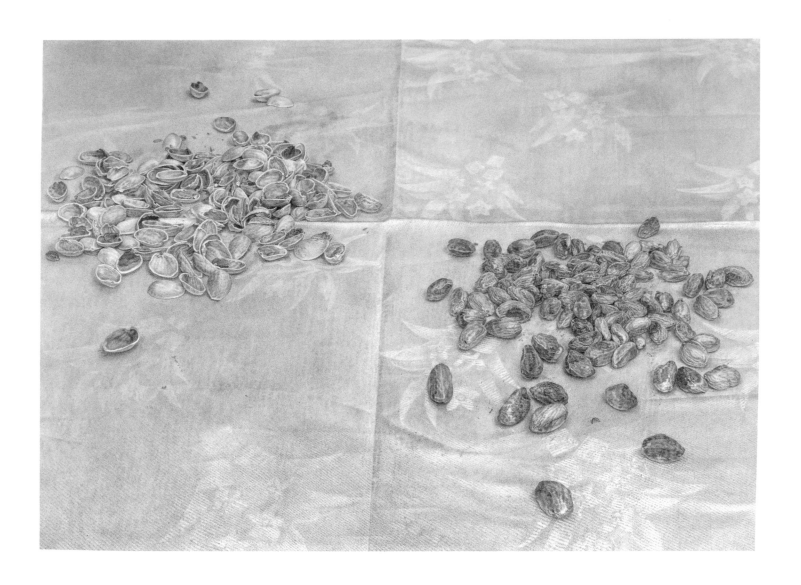

Catherine Murphy

New Work

MAY 1–AUGUST 1, 2008

ESSAY BY JOHN YAU

Knoedler & Company

— ESTABLISHED 1846 —

19 East 70 Street New York New York 10021

Tel 212 794-0550 Fax 212 772-6932

WWW.KNOEDLERGALLERY.COM

Blankets, 2006, oil on canvas, 58 x 84 inches

Hedonist of The Ordinary

I.

Real innovation is rare in any art form, but it seems nearly impossible to achieve in realist painting. Haven't we heard countless times that realism was superseded by cubism, abstraction, and photorealism? What more can anyone do in realist painting, where one directly engages with one's immediate surroundings? What lengths would someone have to go to in order to make realism fresh and contemporary? These are the questions that Catherine Murphy both carefully poses and meticulously answers in her tour de force oil paintings and pencil drawings of everyday occurrences. And like all tour de force works, everything that the artist does feels necessary. In their exactitude for registering the different ways the visual and physical realms coincide, from the painting of the nap of a blanket hanging on a clothesline, and through which sunlight is filtering, to the drawing of the play of shadow and light on a split log's ridged bark and decaying, grooved, interior, Murphy subverts photorealism's privileging of the image over materiality, as well as painterly realism's honoring of materiality over sight. By making vision and tactility synonymous in her paintings and drawings, not only does the artist achieve something that is unprecedented in realist painting, but she also infuses her rigorously conceived investigations of the everyday world with an abundance of inventiveness.

In her merging of inventiveness with a formal interest in two distinct ways an individual apprehends reality, sight, and touch, Murphy both distinguishes her work from the five great realists of the preceding generations, Rackstraw Downes, Antonio López Garcia, Rodrigo Moynihan, Sylvia Plimack Mangold, and Isabella Quintanilla, and gains an equal footing with them. What these artists all share, as well as manifest in very different ways, is their scrupulousness; nothing about their chosen subjects is downplayed or neglected. They see everything with equality, intensity, and care, and are primarily motivated by the desire to discover the absolute limits of seeing that they can chronicle in basic, time-honored, art materials.

By making vision and texture synonymous, often in disquieting ways, Murphy successfully challenges the line of thinking that believes that advanced painting culminated in pure opticality, and rid itself of the material realm. As codified by certain art historians and critics, this line of thinking points back to the paintings of Claude Monet as a source, rather than those by Édouard Manet. But it is out of Manet's sharp-eyed observations and the drawings of George Seurat that Murphy evolves and expands upon, particularly the former's trenchant awareness of class and the latter's use of chiaroscuro to define form without resorting to contour lines. Her way of painting owes nothing to either of these artists, however. In fact, her painting is not indebted to French painting, to its tradition of sketchiness, and insistence on the mark and brushstroke. And just to make it clear how far she has gone, her painting is not obliged to the smooth facture on wooden panels that we associate with Northern Renaissance painting. Her method of painting on canvas is something that she was compelled to make up, and in that regard continues the legacy of Jackson Pollock, who had to find his own way of painting. Her work demonstrates that art history is not a single story, but many, and that lineages are not as evident and logical as some observers would have us believe.

Murphy's preoccupation with the material world as the reality we inhabit, as well as a complex social construction that shapes our identity, has led her to reassess many of the historical assumptions we have made about realist and figurative art. In her quest for an exactitude capable of manifesting both the visual and physical, consider the numerous orthodoxies she rigorously rejects—thick paint, contour line, mechanical devices which enable one to turn reality into an image, style as a way of transforming the world into signature descriptions, the reiteration of the idyllic accoutrements we typically equate with a happy, domestic life, and paeans to an unspoiled landscape. If realism's downfall can be traced to its practitioners contentedly restating reassuring subject matter, then Murphy's deep interest in everyday things and what they signify heeds Charles Baudelaire's demand that we pay direct and immediate attention to the fleeting, contingent, and commonplace. She is a painter of modern life.

In rejecting the conventions associated with realism, the photorealist, and the painterly, Murphy deliberately confronts daunting challenges; she must paint or draw what she sees, which is different than relying on a style to depict what you know to be there. At the same time, accuracy is not the point, but the believable fiction that painting can attain. Measurement and placement within the painting's physical limitations are the driving forces. In getting rid of all the stylistic crutches that realism has historically relied upon, and which certainly helped make it moribund, she has to figure out how to make her materials get her from one edge of the composition to the other. She uses neither con-tour lines nor a grid to help her measure or negotiate the surface. And, as her work makes abundantly evident, she must resolve how to make the things she depicts both visual and palpable. The pictorial is not enough, which is a pointed rejoinder to those who believe that the only domain realism can preside over is the graphic. We don't just see the comforter in *Comforter* (2007); we are inclined to believe that we can reach out and touch it, luxuriate in its folds and thicknesses, just as the woman curled up and asleep appears to be doing. The constant tension between seeing and touching suggests that the different and at times conflicting ways we rec-ognize the physical world we inhabit is one of the artist's central fixations.

By applying thin layers of paint and drawing in pencil, without relying on a contour line, Murphy simultaneously sees and feels her way across the surface. The uncanny way she simultaneously registers the visual and the tactile conveys two divergent ways the individual learns to experience real-ity, the optical acuteness of an adult and the highly sensitive skin of an infant who firsts sees only light and dark. The integration of the visual and tactile is what her paintings and drawings share. Instead of depicting images, she brings us into close visual contact with palpable things. While it may have once been radical for an artist to be true to his or her materials (oil paint and pencil), it has become far more radical to be true to reality, which, according to some theorists, has become inaccessible. It is the seem-ing impossibility of what Murphy has set out to do, which is to provoke viewers to reexamine their visual, physical, philosophical, and social rela-tionships to that which is familiar, that makes it worthy of doing.

In order to be faithful to the material world, where things are both

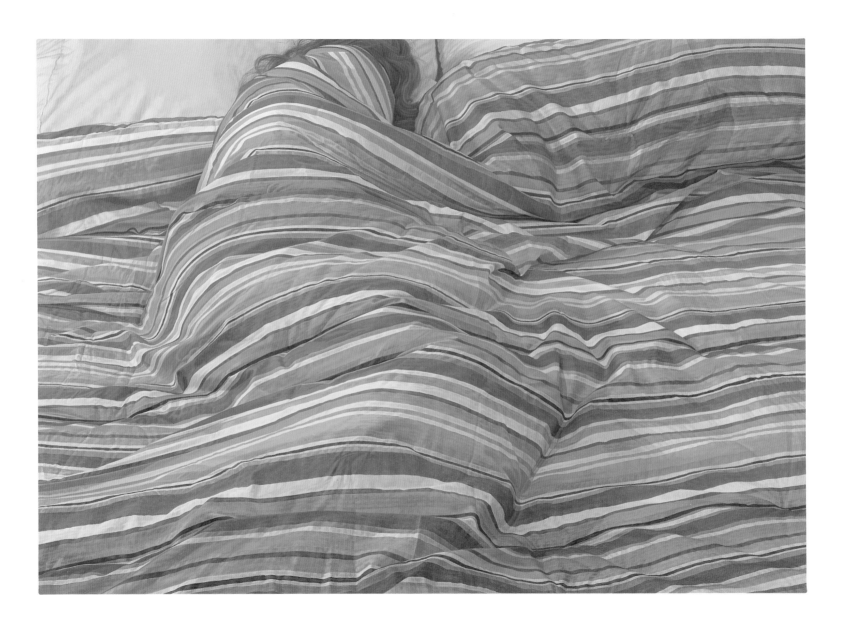

Comforter, 2007, oil on canvas, 54 x 72 inches

distinct forms and overt surfaces, Murphy has developed a practice of painting and drawing that subverts all the conventions associated with realism. She purposefully and often radically changes the scale of her subject matter, defines views that are synonymous with her supports (this is particularly evident when her subject is a window, as in *Xmas Lights*, 2007), and intentionally implicates the viewer (looking down, up, or through, we are always an invisible figure inside the boundaries evoked by the ordinary world manifested in her work). By bringing us into close contact with her subject matter, and ostensibly making us both a witness and narrator in the highly precise yet open-ended event she defines, Murphy is able to interrogate our relationship to the commonplace, to those things that are signs of our self-image.

As implicated viewers, we ask: Who is bent over and looking into the oven? Who has made the cake and what is it for? Who has broken the glass and spilled the milk? And who is going to clean it up? Who is sitting by the window, looking into the night, during the Christmas season? Even when she is painting a window, that portal of possible escape from time's vicissitudes, Murphy doesn't offer us solace from the material world, doesn't relieve us from a nagging awareness of time and mortality. We are staring into the darkness and we feel alone. The festive lights framing the window (and they do glow in the dark) seem remote from our introspective gaze. The feeling of isolation running through her work isn't autobiographical, but common to us all. We see ourselves looking at her work, and perhaps we even gain further insight into the fundamental nature of our inescapable solitude.

II.

Since 2005, which is the last time the artist had a solo exhibition of paintings and drawings[1] in New York, she has completed seven paintings and four large pencil drawings, all of which are included in this exhibition. Building upon the work in that exhibition, the subjects the artist explores in her work of the past four years include a close-up view of a gold-plated crucifix hanging between a woman's ample breasts, a multi-paneled view of a squirrel approaching a sapling in the snow, and photographs torn from a teen magazine and tacked to an adolescent girl's bedroom wall. While a cross of some kind (either as a physical thing or as structuring device) is present in these three paintings, each defines a different way of seeing and negotiating reality. In *Her Bedroom Wall* (2006), where four pages from a teenage girl's fanzine have been pushed to the painting's four corners, so that each image is only partially seen; and in *Surveillance* (2007), a four-panel painting of a squirrel, the absence or space where nothing has been put forms a cross, dividing the painting into quadrants, which are related to, as well as distinct from, each other. Here, we see the artist has fully absorbed structuring devices associated with abstract art, but never with the intent to parody or belittle them. Rather, she reminds us that we shape our seeing, that it is always mediated in one way or another, and that the borders separating such categories as realism and abstraction are porous. *Her Bedroom Wall* and *Surveillance* are both realist and abstract.

In addition to dividing the surface, as well as helping to define form and surface, the quadrants are cropped by the work's physical edges, so that the view (or what is contained within the painting) is simultaneously partial and dependent upon our presence. By implying that we are in the painting, and witnessing the commonplace episode, Murphy is able to make us become the individual watching the squirrel become visible on a surveillance camera or someone looking at, but not completely seeing, the cheap images ripped from a magazine. The tension between the slightly crumpled, torn pages and the idealized magazine reproductions is just one of the pressures enlivening the painting.

In the drawing *Oven Light* (2008), we have opened the oven door and are bending down and looking at a cake sitting in its round, nine-inch pan. Looking is always an action connected to our physical body. In our mind's eye, we have to physically realign our bodies in order to understand our relationship to the drawing. We are not just looking, we are conscious of our implied physical position as we scrutinize the work, often in conditions that make us highly self-conscious about the nature of our curiosity. What is it that we are hoping to learn? Into what forbidden zone has our looking taken us? The implied confines of looking, which are a result of the artist's highly considered structuring of the physical, visual, and social, instill another emotional edge into her commonplace experiences.

In *Blankets* (2006), we are peering at two half-seen figures through two red blankets hanging on a clothesline, while in *Pendant* (2005), we are staring at a crucifix nestled in the veined cleavage of a woman's abundant breasts. Both paintings turn us into voyeurs, but in very different ways. In *Blankets*, we want to know what is transpiring on the other side of the blankets, as well as wonder why we are outside this community. Are we a stranger who is spying on these unsuspecting individuals, who seem as if they are about to become lovers, or are we just the third wheel? An ordinary event has become fraught with possibilities, all of which are authored by us. This is complicated further by the tactility of the blanket and the partial view of the two people seated on the other side; they are in their own world. In *Blankets*, tactility, which implies intimacy, and vision, which implies distance, circle each other like dancers who never come together.

In *Pendant*, the tightly cropped, close-up, frontal view suggests that we have become a child of unspecified sex who is standing close to (or is possibly even being held by) a full-bodied woman who is taller than us, and whose face we do not see and thus cannot identify. The proximity of our body to hers, and the particular view the painting brings into sharp focus, causes us to become extremely self-conscious. Are we about to be hugged by her? Is this the kind of dress a woman should be wearing when hugging a pre-adolescent child? Is she a relative, a family friend, someone we hardly know, or a complete stranger? Is this view something that we (as children) are apt to experience while standing on a crowded bus, subway, or elevator? Or, if we go in a completely different direction, is this woman stripped down to her bra? And if so, who are we? Running smoothly through all of these questions is another set of queries; is she being prurient or are we being prudes? The tension between seeing the lambent crucifix and the tactility of the breasts and veined skin animates the entire painting. Structurally, the curve of the neckline becomes an inverted arch, which makes the painting more secular than spiritual. There is no heaven above, only an unseen face. The scale of the subject matter to the framing edges brings the viewer into a zone of possible intimacy that the artist refuses to categorize as private or public. She could be standing in a bedroom or on a busy street. A commonplace sight—a woman wearing a crucifix—becomes strange and provocative, discomfiting and profane.

One of Murphy's singular accomplishments is the realm of self-consciousness she establishes for the viewer to enter and reflect upon; she investigates views that are familiar, but are most likely aspects of our experience that we have either downplayed or haven't stopped to consider. These features include class, the inescapable forces which shape our identity, and the fact that we are all caught in time. In *Pendant*, the discrepancy between our implied size and that of the woman raises all sorts of unsettling questions. Is wearing a crucifix one of the ways girls learn to inhabit their sexual body? What does it mean to wear a figure of a dead man close to your heart? Is there some significance to the fact that a woman is literally carrying and to some degree shielding a man on a cross? A familiar sight no longer seems benign or even full of goodwill.

Pendant extends and redefines a perceptual realm that originates with Manet's *Olympia* (1863), a prostitute who is unashamed of putting herself on display. Isn't Murphy's largely unseen woman doing something very similar, but within a bigger, and perhaps more public circumstance? The difference is that Manet evoked the unspoken barriers separating men and women, and the advantaged and disadvantaged, in 19th century Paris, while Murphy is getting at something more insidious though no less powerful; what role does religious upbringing play in the way women learn to identify themselves?

Although more than a century separates them, both Manet and Murphy understand why it is necessary to be blasphemous. God may be

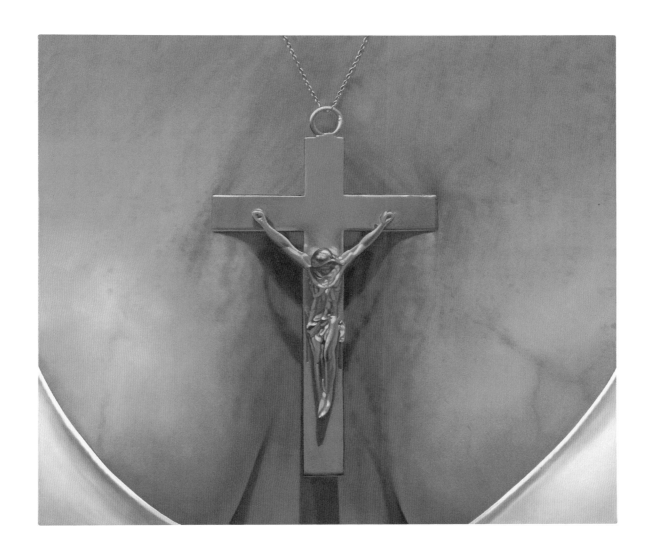

Pendant, 2005, oil on canvas, 42 x 47 3/4 inches

dead, but surely the events of the past fifty years, both nationally and internationally, have made it painfully clear that a significant number of the world's population maintain a fanatical belief in a higher authority. At the very least, this suggests that many of us never fully leave our childhood behind. Like Manet, Murphy's impoliteness reveals the rifts separating us into distinct classes, whose members are governed willingly, and not so willingly, by a set of foregone conclusions. By making us intimate witnesses, something that Manet also did in *Olympia*, we are asked to reflect upon our own prejudices and inclinations about others who have arrived at a very different set of conclusions than the ones each of us has reached. Have we even stopped to consider what foregone conclusions we have reached? And do our judgments make us better, and more informed, than others? Why do we believe this is so? Is it because we have some purchase on the *Truth*?

What *Pendant* reminds me of—and here I am speaking of those both in the art world and not in it—is that we all believe that we are members of a colony of the saved (even if that colony consists of only one member), but we seldom admit that the relationship with other colonies is constantly fractious, and that conflagrations of one intensity or another are always ready to spread. I cannot think of another realist painter who recognizes how deeply imbedded volatility has become in our social fabric. The fact that Murphy uses ordinary events to arrive at this insight is foreboding, to say the least.

III.
I have briefly touched upon the very different kinds of looking that

Murphy examines in her paintings and drawings. For her, there is no such thing as an innocent bystander. We are spying on a squirrel, an unwanted rodent interloper, with a surveillance camera. What do we plan to do next? Whether we are conscious of it or not, we are always engaged with reality, even when we are asleep, like the woman in *Comforter*. It isn't only what we see, but how we see and judge it, that Murphy explores with immense sympathy, particularly from the point of view of those for whom art probably has little importance.

In having us feel as if we are looking into an oven, at a new, still creased tablecloth covered with nuts and shells, a broken glass of spilled milk, and a split, decaying log, the artist reminds us that no matter what social position we have attained or inherited, we still make, consume, and waste— that these actions are intrinsic to our lives. Instead of designating others to be responsible for what is necessary, particularly the making and cleaning-up, so that we can simply go on consuming, Murphy wants us to recognize their inseparability. That she reaches these experiences through the most rudimentary means, pencil and paper, and without relying on conventional techniques (or what might be called shortcuts), ought to serve as an aesthetic, moral, and political lesson for us all. The immense and particular cornucopia of pleasures that she offers us in her paintings and drawings is something that we should consider carefully. We are not meant to consume her art without reflection.

— John Yau

1. *Catherine Murphy: Paintings & Drawings 2001– 2004*, Lennon, Weinberg, Inc., New York, February 9–March 19, 2005. The exhibition included eight oil paintings and five large graphite drawings that the artist completed between 2002 and 2004.

Her Bedroom Wall, 2006, oil on canvas, 56 x 56 inches

Surveillance, 2007, oil on canvas, 4 panels, each 30 x 30 inches

Xmas Lights, 2007, oil on canvas, 52 x 59 1/2 inches
Collection of Emily Leland Todd

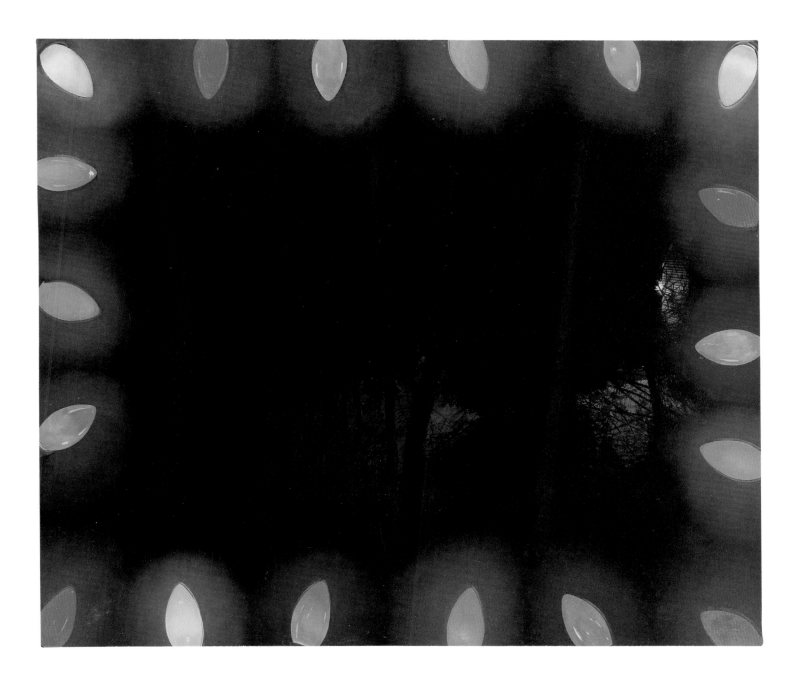

Hand Mirror, 2008, oil on canvas, 46 x 54 1/2 inches

Split, 2007, graphite on paper, 36 x 42 1/2 inches
Collection of Maxine and Stuart Frankel Foundation for Art, Bloomfield Hills, Michigan

Spill, 2007, graphite on paper, 28 x 40 inches
Private collection

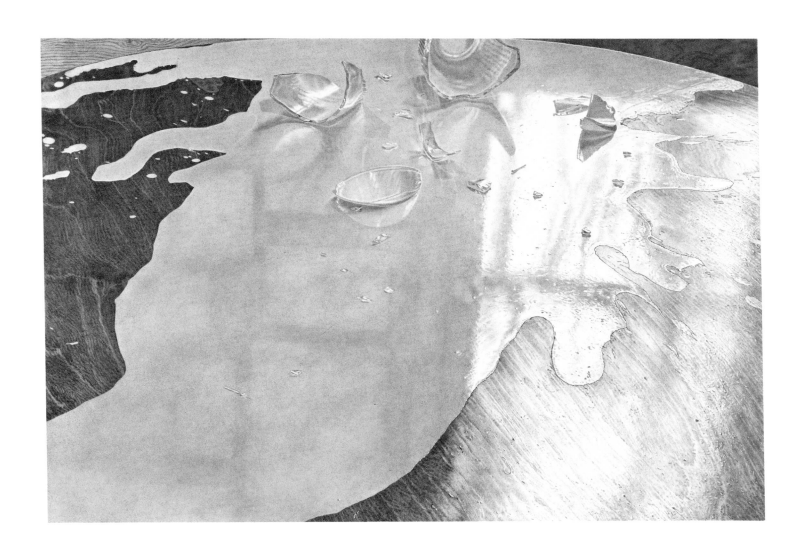

Oven Light, 2008, graphite on paper, 29 5/8 x 37 inches

CATHERINE MURPHY

Born, Cambridge, Massachusetts, 1946
Resides and works in Poughkeepsie, New York

Education

1966   Skowhegan School of Painting and Sculpture
1967   B.F.A., Pratt Institute, Brooklyn

Awards and Grants

1979   National Endowment for the Arts
1982   Guggenheim Fellowship
1986   Ingram Merrill Foundation Grant
1989   National Endowment for the Arts
1990   Award in Art, American Academy and Institute of Arts
        and Letters
2000   Anonymous Was A Woman
2002   Member, American Academy and Institute of Arts and
        Letters
2006   Honorary Doctorate, Pratt Institute

Teaching

1989–Present Yale University, New Haven, Senior Critic

Solo Exhibitions

1972   *Catherine Murphy: Paintings,* First Street Gallery, New
        York.
        Piper Gallery, Lexington.
1975   *Catherine Murphy: Recent Paintings*, Fourcade, Droll, Inc.,
        New York.
1976   *Catherine Murphy: Paintings, Drawings, Lithographs,* The
        Phillips Collection, Washington, DC. Traveled to Institute of
        Contemporary Art, Boston. Catalogue with text by Judith
        Hoos.

1979   *Catherine Murphy: Recent Paintings*, Xavier Fourcade, Inc.,
        New York.
1985   *Catherine Murphy: New Paintings and Drawings, 1980–1985*,
        Xavier Fourcade, Inc., New York. Catalogue with text by
        Linda Nochlin.
1988   *Catherine Murphy, Paintings and Drawings*, J. Rosenthal
        Fine Arts, Ltd., Chicago.
1989   *Catherine Murphy: New Paintings and Drawings*, Lennon,
        Weinberg, Inc., New York. Catalogue with text by Jill
        Weinberg and Bernard Lennon.
1992   *Catherine Murphy*, Lennon, Weinberg, Inc., New York.
1994–95 *Catherine Murphy, Her World*, Greenville County Museum
        of Art, Greenville, South Carolina.
1995   *Catherine Murphy: Works on Paper 1980–95*, Lennon,
        Weinberg, Inc., New York.
        Catherine Murphy: Paintings 1992–95, Lennon,
        Weinberg, Inc., New York.
1998   Baumgartner Galleries, Washington, DC.
        Catherine Murphy: New Work, Lennon, Weinberg, Inc.,
        New York.
1999   *Catherine Murphy: Paintings*, Texas Gallery, Houston.
2001   *Catherine Murphy: Paintings and Drawings 1999–2001,*
        Lennon, Weinberg, Inc., New York.
2002   *Catherine Murphy: Paintings & Drawings*, Daniel Weinberg
        Gallery, Los Angeles.
2005   *Catherine Murphy: Paintings & Drawings 2001–2004,*
        Lennon, Weinberg, Inc., New York.
2006   *Catherine Murphy,* Texas Gallery, Houston.
2008   *Catherine Murphy: New Work,* Knoedler & Company,
        New York.

Group Exhibitions

1971   *The Contemporary Figure: A New Realism,* Suffolk
        Museum, Stony Brook.
        Landscape II, DeCordova Museum and Sculpture Park,
        Lincoln. Catalogue with text by Frederick P. Walkey.
1972   Prince Street Gallery, New York.
        Women in Art, J. L. Hudson Gallery, Detroit.
        Landscape, The Museum of Modern Art, Art Lending
        Services, New York.

1972   *Contemporary American Painting, 1972 Annual Exhibition,* Whitney Museum of American Art, New York.

1972–73 *The Realist Revival,* American Federation of Arts, New York. Traveling. Catalogue with text by Scott Burton.

1973   The Benson Gallery, Bridgehampton.
The Parrish Art Museum, Southampton.
New American Landscapes, Vassar College Art Gallery, Poughkeepsie. Catalogue with text by Margaret Nesbit.
A Sense of Place: The Artist and the American Landscape, Sheldon Memorial Art Gallery, Lincoln. Traveled to Joslyn Art Museum, Omaha.
Painting in America: Yesterday and Tomorrow, Decorative Arts Center, New York.
Biennial Exhibition. Whitney Museum of American Art, New York.
Painting and Sculpture 1973, The Emerging Real, Storm King Art Center, Mountainville.
Choice Dealers—Dealer's Choice, New York Cultural Center, New York.

1974   *New Images: Figuration in American Painting,* Queens Museum of Art, New York. Catalogue.
Woman's Work: American Art 1974, Museum of the Philadelphia Civic Center.
Collectors Gallery VIII, Marion Koogler McNay Art Museum, San Antonio.
Painting and Sculpture Today—1974. Indianapolis Museum of Art.
Weatherspoon Art Gallery, University of North Carolina at Greensboro.
In Her Own Image, Samuel S. Fleisher Memorial, Philadelphia, in conjunction with the Philadelphia Museum of Art. Organized by Cindy Nemser. Traveled through the Smithsonian Institution Exhibition Services.

1975   *New Images in American Figurative Painting,* Squibb Gallery, Princeton.
Portrait Painting 1970–1975: A Survey of Informal Portraiture in the USA, Alan Frumkin Gallery, New York.
Candid Painting: American Genre 1950–1975, DeCordova Museum and Sculpture Park, Lincoln. Catalogue with text by Eva Jacob.

1976   *A Selection of American Art: The Skowhegan School, 1946–1976,* Institute of Contemporary Art, Boston. Traveled to Colby College Museum of Art, Waterville, Maine. Catalogue.

1976–78 *Artists Choice: Figurative Art in New York,* Green Mountain, Bowery, Prince Street, First Street Galleries, and Soho Center for Visual Artists, New York.

1977   *Contemporary Issues: Works on Paper by Women,* The Woman's Building, Los Angeles.
Works on Paper, Small Format, Objects: Duchamp to Heizer, Xavier Fourcade, Inc., New York.
A View of a Decade, Museum of Contemporary Art, Chicago. Catalogue with text by Martin Friedman, Robert Pincus-Witten, and Peter Gay.
Artists Salute Skowhegan, Kennedy Galleries, New York. Catalogue.

1978   *Perspective '78: Works by Women,* Freedman Gallery, Albright College, Reading. Catalogue.

1979   *Awards Exhibition,* American Academy and Institute of Arts and Letters, New York.
16 Realistas, Centro Colombo Americano, Bogotá. Catalogue with text by Jaime Manrique Ardila.

1980   *Small Scale: Paintings, Drawings, Sculpture,* Xavier Fourcade, Inc., New York.
Exchanges II, Henry Street Settlement House, New York.
Aspects of the 70's, Directions in Realism, Danforth Museum of Art, Framingham. Catalogue with text by John Perreault.
Contemporary Naturalism: Works of the 1970's, Nassau County Museum of Art, Roslyn Harbor. Catalogue with text by Lawrence Alloway.
American Drawings in Black and White, Brooklyn Museum.
Artist's Choice—Younger Artists, Fischbach Gallery, New York. Organized by The Artists' Choice Museum.
One Major New Work Each, Xavier Fourcade, Inc., New York.
American Academy and Institute of Arts and Letters, New York.

1981   *The Americans: The Landscape,* Contemporary Arts Museum, Houston.
The Contemporary American Landscape, Hirschl & Adler, New York.
The Image in American Painting and Sculpture 1950–1980, Akron Art Museum.

1981–82 *Real, Really Real and Super Real: Directions in Contemporary American Realism,* San Antonio Museum of Art. Traveled to

Indianapolis Museum of Art; Tucson Museum of Art; Museum of Art, Carnegie Institute, Pittsburgh. Catalogue with text by Alvin Martin and Linda Nochlin.
Contemporary American Realism, Pennsylvania Academy of the Fine Arts, Philadelphia. Traveled to Virginia Museum of Fine Arts, Richmond; Oakland Museum. Catalogue with text by Frank H. Goodyear, Jr.

1982   *Women's Art, Miles Apart*, Aaron Berman Gallery, New York. Traveled to Valencia Community College, Orlando.
Lower Manhattan From Street to Sky, Whitney Museum of American Art, East Campus Gallery, Downtown at Federal Reserve Plaza, New York.
Architectural Images: Contemporary Paintings, Summit Art Center. Catalogue with text by Meg Raftis.
Modern American Painting: Museum of Fine Arts, Houston, National Pinakothiki, Athens. Traveled to Museum of Fine Arts, Houston.

1982–83   *Contemporary Realist Painting: A Selection*, Museum of Fine Arts, Boston.
Perspectives on Contemporary American Realism: Works of Art on Paper from the Collection of Jalane and Richard Davidson, Pennsylvania Academy of the Fine Arts, Philadelphia. Traveled to the Art Institute of Chicago. Catalogue.

1983   *Printed by Women: A National Exhibition of Photographs and Prints*, The Print Club, Port of History Museum at Penn's Landing, Philadelphia. Catalogue.
New York, New Work: Contemporary Painting from New York Galleries, Delaware Art Museum, Wilmington.
Drawings, Xavier Fourcade, Inc., New York.

1983–84   *In Honor of de Kooning*, Xavier Fourcade, Inc., New York. Catalogue.
American Still Life: 1945–1983, Contemporary Arts Museum, Houston. Traveled to Albright-Knox Art Gallery, Buffalo; Columbus Museum of Art; Neuberger Museum of Art, Purchase College, State University of New York; Portland Art Museum. Catalogue.

1984   *The Artists' Choice Museum: The First Eight Years*, Artists' Choice Museum, New York.
Art on Paper 1984, the 20th Weatherspoon Annual Exhibition, Weatherspoon Art Museum, University of North Carolina at Greensboro. Catalogue.

American Still Life, 1945–1983, Neuberger Museum of Art, Purchase College, State University of New York.
Recent American Still Life, Robert Schoelkopf Gallery, New York.

1985   *Variation on a Theme: Figurative Painting*, Brainerd Art Gallery, Potsdam College, State University of New York.
American Realism: The Precise Image, The Isetan Museum of Art, Tokyo. Traveled to The Diamaru Museum, Osaka; Yokohama Takashimaya. Catalogue.

1985–86   *The New Response: Contemporary Painters of the Hudson River*, Albany Institute of History and Art. Traveled to Vassar College Art Gallery, Poughkeepsie; The Artists' Choice Museum, New York. Catalogue.

1986   *Members' Drawings*, Hirschl & Adler, New York, in association with The Drawings Society, New York. Catalogue.

1986–87   *American Realism: Twentieth Century Drawings and Watercolors*, San Francisco Museum of Modern Art. Traveled to DeCordova Museum and Sculpture Park, Lincoln; Archer M. Huntington Art Gallery, Austin; Mary and Leigh Block Gallery, Evanston; Williams College Museum of Art, Williamstown; Akron Art Museum; Madison Art Center. Catalogue.
The Window in Twentieth Century Art, Neuberger Museum of Art, Purchase College, State University of New York. Traveled to Contemporary Arts Museum, Houston. Catalogue.
Boston Collects: Contemporary Painting and Sculpture, Museum of Fine Arts, Boston. Catalogue with text by Theodore E. Stebbins, Jr. and Judith Hoos Fox.

1987   *Drawings*, Xavier Fourcade, Inc., New York.
Paintings and Sculptures by Candidates for Art Awards, American Academy and Institute of Arts and Letters, New York.
Paintings, Xavier Fourcade, Inc., New York.
In Memory of Xavier Fourcade: A Group Exhibition, Xavier Fourcade, Inc., New York.
39th Annual Academy: Institute Purchase Exhibition, American Academy and Institute of Arts and Letters, New York.

1989   *Group Exhibition*, Lennon, Weinberg, Inc., New York.
Making Their Mark: Women Artists Move Into the Mainstream 1970–1985, Cincinnati Art Museum. Traveled to

New Orleans Museum of Fine Art; Denver Art Museum; Pennsylvania Academy of The Fine Arts, Philadelphia. Catalogue.

Paintings and Sculpture, Lennon, Weinberg, Inc., New York.

Works on Paper, Lennon, Weinberg, Inc., New York.

A Decade of American Drawings 1980–1989, Daniel Weinberg Gallery, Los Angeles.

41st Annual Academy-Institute Purchase Exhibition, American Academy and Institute of Arts and Letters, New York.

1990   *A Group Exhibition*, Lennon, Weinberg, Inc., New York.

Persistence of Vision, Tibor de Nagy Gallery, New York.

Distinguished Visiting Artist in Residence 1990 Exhibition, Watkins Gallery, American University, Washington, DC.

Academy-Institute Invitational Exhibition of Painting and Sculpture, New York, American Academy and Institute of Arts and Letters, New York.

Exhibition of Work by Newly Elected Members and Recipients of Awards, American Academy and Institute of Arts and Letters, New York.

Drawings, Lennon, Weinberg, Inc., New York.

Landscape Painting 1960–1990: The Italian Tradition in American Art, Gibbes Museum of Art, Charleston; University of Virginia Art Museum, Charlottesville. Catalogue with text by John Hollander.

Black and White: Works on Paper, Linda Cathcart Gallery, Santa Monica.

Group Exhibition of Gallery Artists, Lennon, Weinberg, Inc., New York.

Contemporary American Still Lifes in Motion, Wilson Arts Center, Rochester.

42nd Annual Academy-Institute Purchase Exhibition, American Academy and Institute of Arts and Letters, New York.

New Faculty Exhibition, A & A Gallery, Yale School of Art, Yale University, New Haven.

1990–91   *Art on Paper 1990*, Weatherspoon Art Museum, University of North Carolina at Greensboro.

1991   *Exquisite Paintings*, Orlando Museum of Art. Catalogue with text by Gerrit Henry.

Spring/Summer Exhibition, Part One: Painters, Lennon, Weinberg, Inc., New York.

Against the Grain: Images in American Art, 1960–1990, Southern Alleghenies Museum of Art, Loretto. Catalogue with text by Paul Binai.

Beyond the Picturesque: Landscape on Paper, G.W. Einstein Company, Inc., New York.

1991–92   *American Realism and Figurative Art 1952–1991*, Miyaqui Museum of Art, Sendai. Traveled to Soqo Museum of Art, Yokohama; The Tokushima Modern Art Museum; The Museum of Modern Art, Shiga; Kochi Prefectural Museum of Folk Art. Catalogue.

1992   *Beyond Realism, Image and Enigma*, Southern Alleghenies Museum of Art, Loretto. Catalogue.

44th Annual Academy-Institute Purchase Exhibition, American Academy and Institute of Arts and Letters, New York.

1993   *Artists by Artists*, Forum Gallery, New York.

Keny Gallery, Columbus.

Works on Paper by Gallery Artists, Lennon, Weinberg, Inc., New York.

Drawings III, Koplin Gallery, Santa Monica.

Interior Outlook, The Gallery at Hastings-on-Hudson, Municipal Building.

1994   *Drawing on Friendship: Portraits of Painters and Poets*, Tibor de Nagy Gallery, New York. Traveled to Reynolds Gallery, Richmond.

Gallery Artists, Lennon, Weinberg, Inc., New York.

An Original Idea: Realist Drawings, Wunderlich & Co., New York.

Inspired by Nature, Neuberger Museum of Art, Purchase College, State University of New York.

Novices Collect: Selections from the Sam and May Gruber Collection, The Currier Gallery of Art, Manchester. Catalogue.

Songs of the Earth: Twenty-two American Painters of the Landscape, AHI Gallery, New York.

New York Realism—Past and Present, Tampa Museum of Art. Traveled to Odakyo Art Museum, Tokyo; Kagoshima Museum of Art; Kitakyushu Municipal Museum of Art; The Museum of Art, Kintetsu, Osaka; Fukushima Prefectural Museum of Art. Catalogue with text by Douglas Dreishpoon and Jennifer Gross.

1995   *Still Life and "Feminine" Space*, Contemporary Realist Gallery, San Francisco, California.
1995 Biennial, Whitney Museum of American Art, New York.
Gallery Artists, Lennon, Weinberg, Inc., New York.
American Interiors, Knoedler & Company, New York.
Nature Studies I, University Gallery, Fine Arts Center, University of Massachusetts, Amherst.
Faculty Work on Paper, Yale University School of Art Gallery, New Haven.

1996   *On Paper*, Marlborough Galleries, New York. Traveled to Galeria Marlborough, Madrid.
Reality Bites: Realism in Contemporary Art, Kemper Museum of Contemporary Art, Kansas City. Catalogue with text by Barbara Bloemink and Dana Self.
Rediscovering the Landscape of the Americas, Gerald Peters Gallery, Santa Fe. Catalogue with text by Alan Gussow.

1996–98 *Objects of Personal Significance*, Exhibits USA, Mid-Atlantic Arts Alliance, Kansas City. Traveled. Catalogue with text by Janet Marquardt-Cherry.

1997   *Masterworks: New York on Paper*, Baumgartner Galleries, Washington, DC.
Feminine Image, Nassau County Museum of Art, Roslyn Harbor. Catalogue with text by Donald Kuspit.

1997–98 *Still Life: The Object in American Art 1915–1995: Selections from The Metropolitan Museum of Art*, organized by the American Federation of Arts, New York. Traveled to Marsh Art Gallery, Richmond; The Arkansas Art Center, Little Rock; New York State Museum, Albany; Newport Harbor Art Museum, Newport Beach; Philbrook Museum of Art, Tulsa; The Society of the Four Arts, Palm Beach; Salina Art Center.
Landscape, Seen and Unseen, Pratt Manhattan Gallery, New York.

1998   *Landscapes*, Meyerson & Nowinski, Seattle.
Original Scale, Apex Art, New York. John Yau, curator.
Food Matters, Bucknell Center Gallery, Lewisburg.
UTZ: A Collected Exhibition, Lennon, Weinberg, Inc., New York.
Beyond the Mountain: American Landscape Today, Asheville Art Museum.
The Risk of Existence, Phyllis Kind Gallery, New York.

1999   *Catherine Murphy, Joan Mitchell, Harriet Korman: Three Rooms*, Lennon, Weinberg, Inc., New York.

1999–   *Beyond the Mountains: the Contemporary American*
2000   *Landscape*, Newcomb Gallery, Tulane University, New Orleans. Traveled to Muskegon Museum of Art; Polk Museum of Art, Lakeland; Boise Art Museum; Fort Wayne Museum of Art; The Lyman Allyn Museum, New London.
Green Wood and Crystal Waters: The American Landscape Tradition Since 1950, The Philbrook Museum of Art, Tulsa. Traveled to John and Mable Ringling Museum of Art, Sarasota.

2000   *Conceptual Realism*, Rosenwald-Wolf Gallery, The University of the Arts, Philadelphia. Catalogue with text by Sid Sachs.
The Likeness of Being: Contemporary Self Portraits by 60 Women Artists, D.C. Moore Gallery, New York.
Insites: Interior Spaces in Contemporary Art, Whitney Museum of American Art at Champion, Stamford.
The Figure: Another Side of Moderninsm, Snug Harbor Cultural Center, Inc., Staten Island, New York.
Inside Out: the Space of Landscape + Architecture, Lobby Gallery, Harvard University, Cambridge.

2001   *At Home*, Lennon, Weinberg, Inc., New York.
Uncommon Threads: Contemporary Artists and Clothing, Herbert F. Johnson Museum of Art, Cornell University, Ithaca. Catalogue with text by Sean M. Ulmer.

2002   *The Perception of Appearance*, Frye Art Museum, Seattle.
Some Options in Realism, Carpenter Center, Harvard University, Cambridge. Catalogue with text by Klaus Kertess.
Painting: a passionate response, Seventeen Artists, The Painting Center, New York.
Proximity, The Work Space, New York. Catalogue with text by Hearne Pardee.

2003   *Mighty Graphitey,* Feature, Inc., New York.

2004   *Toys in the Attic*, Lennon, Weinberg, Inc., New York.
Group Show, Lennon, Weinberg, Inc., New York.

2005   *This Must Be the Place*, Center for Curatorial Studies, Bard College, Annandale-on-Hudson.
Group Exhibition: Gallery Artists, Lennon, Weinberg, Inc., New York.

2005–06 *The Obligation to Endure: Art & Ecology Since Silent Spring*, The New York Academy of Sciences, New York.

2006   *Men,* I-20 Gallery, New York. Eileen Altfest, curator.

2007   *All the More Real: Portrayals of Intimacy and Empathy,* The Parrish Art Museum, Southampton. Catalogue with essays by Merrill Falkenberg, Eric Fischl, and John Haskell.

2008   *Here's the Thing: The Single Object Still Life,* Katonah Museum of Art. Robert Cottingham, curator. Catalogue.

Bibliography

Mila André. "Off the path, and well worth the trip," *New York Daily News* (March 23, 1990).

Anonymous. "Artist's brush alters 'homely' landscapes," *Lexington Minute-Man* (March 13, 1975).

_____. "Art: Catherine Murphy," *The New Yorker* (April 13, 1992).

_____. "Images of Nature," *Scholastic Art* 23, no. 3 (December 1992–January 1993).

_____. "*Still Life* the Focus of State Museum Exhibit," *The Post-Star, Glens Falls, New York* (May 28, 1998).

_____. "Catherine Murphy," *The New Yorker* (May 11, 1998).

_____. "Houston's Texas Gallery Shows New York Painter's Work," *The Big Bend Sentinel* (February 11, 1999).

_____. "The Mundane Turns Strange," *Los Angeles Times* (December 6, 2002).

John Arthur. *Spirit of Place: Contemporary Landscape Painting and the American Tradition* (Boston: Bulfinch Press, Little, Brown and Co., 1989).

Alan G. Artner. "Murphy's Clearly Focused Realism Makes No Excuses," *Chicago Tribune* (November 25, 1988).

Kenneth Baker. "The View from Catherine Murphy's Window," *The Boston Phoenix* (May 11, 1976).

Ruth Bass. "New York? New York!," *Art-Talk* [Scottsdale, Arizona] (January 1990).

Wendy Beckett. *Contemporary Women Artists* (New York: Universe, 1988).

Byron Belt. "Special Exhibit of Art By Women," *Springfield Sunday Republican* (March 19, 1989).

Meryle Beveridge. "Galleries," *The Washington Post* (March 2, 1976).

_____. "Calendar Art," *The Washington Star* (March 7, 1976).

David Bourdon. "Art: Cityscapes," *Architectural Digest* (September 1978).

_____. "Critic's Diary: Seeing It All, or Six Weeks in Manhattan Galleries," *Art in America* (September 1992).

John Canaday. "Suffolk Museum Offering Display," *The New York Times* (September 19, 1971).

_____. "Only Half Bad—And That's Half Good," *The New York Times* (February 6, 1972).

David Carrier. "Turku: Soviet Art of the Stalin Era," *Burlington Magazine* (August 1995).

Andrea Coddington. "Figuratively Speaking," *Art & Auction* (June 1996).

Mark Daniel Cohen. "Catherine Murphy," *Review* (May 1, 1998).

Sarah Booth Conroy. "The Vice President's Residence: Eagles, Hopper and Ernst," *Artnews* (November 1975).

Roger Downey. "Face Time: The Frye Looks Ahead for Figures," *Seattle Weekly* (July 25, 2002).

Peter Eleey. "Catherine Murphy: Lennon, Weinberg," *The Brooklyn Rail* (January–February 2002).

Allen Ellenzweig. "Catherine Murphy," *Arts Magazine* (February 1975).

Alicia Faxon. "Painting Reality," *The Real Paper* [Boston] (May 23, 1976).

Richard J. Flanson, III and Tress Ruslander Miller. *The Security Pacific Collection 1970–1985: Selected Works* (Los Angeles: Security Pacific, 1985).

Robert Garrett. "Let's Look at Problem *Realistically,* "*Boston Herald American* (May 2, 1976).

Nancy Grimes. "Facts of Life," *Artnews* (December 1988).

John Gruen. "Catherine Murphy: The Rise of a Cult Figure," *Artnews* (December 1978).

_____. "Catherine Murphy," *The Artist Observed: 28 Interviews with Contemporary Artists* (Chicago: A Cappella Books, 1991).

_____. "The Magic of the Commonplace," *Quest/80* (January 1980).

Barbara Hagstrom. "Canvas Reality," *Dutchess* (Summer 1988).

Piri Halasz. "Painter with a Novelist's Eye," *The New York Times* (January 11, 1976).

_____. "State Acquires Two Art Works," *The New York Times* (August 11, 1998).

Gerrit Henry. "New York Reviews," *Artnews* (April 1975).

_____. "Catherine Murphy," *Artnews* (March 1986).

_____. "The Figurative Field," *Art in America* (January 1994).

Roberta Hershenson. "The Fine, Painstaking Art of Arranging a Major Exhibition," *The New York Times* (November 9, 1986).

Faye Hirsch. "Catherine Murphy at Lennon, Weinberg," *Art in America* (June/July 2005).

William J. Hrushesky. "Timing is Everything," *The Sciences* (July/August 1994).

Sam Hunter and John Jacobus. *Modern Art: Painting, Sculpture, Architecture*, 3rd ed. (New York: Harry N. Abrams, Inc., 1992).

Ken Johnson. "Big Top Whitney," *Art in America* (June 1995).

_____."Catherine Murphy," *The New York Times* (May 15, 1998).

_____. "Catherine Murphy," *The New York Times* (March 4, 2005).

_____. "Lines, Shapes and Subjects, Lost and Found, That Link the Centuries," *The New York Times* (November 1, 2007).

Susie Kalil. "The American Landscape—Contemporary Interpretations," *Artweek* (April 25, 1981).

_____. "The Good, Long Look," *Houston Press* (February 25–March 3, 1999).

Jason Edward Kaufman. "Do You Remember Realism?" *New York City Tribune* (February 19, 1990).

Klaus Kertess. "Figuring It Out," *Artforum* (November 1980).

Hilton Kramer. "An Uncommon Painter of the Commonplace," *The New York Times* (March 9, 1975).

_____. "Catherine Murphy," *The New York Times* (May 11, 1979).

_____. "Soho: Figures at an Exhibition," *The New York Times* (December 10, 1977).

_____. "Art: Five-Gallery Realist Show," *The New York Times* (September 12, 1980).

_____. "The Real Things," *New York Magazine* (July 16, 1984).

Daniel Kunitz. "Changing Faces," *Artnews* (March 1999).

_____. "Gallery Chronicle," *The New Criterion* (December 2001).

Kay Larson. "The Real Things," *New York Magazine* (July 16, 1984).

_____. "Catherine Murphy," *New York Magazine* (December 16, 1985).

Margarett Loke. "Realism: Catherine Murphy—It Chose Her," *Artnews* (February 1996).

Ellen Lubell. "Manhattan (and Hoboken)," *Soho Weekly News* (May 24–30, 1979).

Edward Lucie-Smith. *American Art Now* (New York: William Morrow & Company, Inc., 1985).

Daniel M. Mendelowitz, David L. Faber, and Duane A. Wakeham. *A Guide to Drawing*, 7th edition (Thomson Wadsworth, 1997).

Margaret Moorman. "Catherine Murphy," *Artnews* (April 1990).

Chris Moylan. "Nostalgia for the Actual," *artcritical.com* (October 2001).

Catherine Murphy. "Art is My Lifestyle," *The Woman Artist* [Special issue of *Art & Man*] 5, no. 2 (November 1974).

Annette Nachumi. "Exchanges II," *Art/World* (May 21–June 18, 1980).

Jean Nathan. "The Transom: The Chosen," *The New York Observer* (March 26, 1990).

Mario Naves. "Up-Close Paintings Ask Us to Back Off, Just a Little," *The New York Observer* (October 15, 2001).

_____. "A Realist's New Paintings Winnowed to Bare Essentials," *The New York Observer* (March 7, 2005).

Ross Neher. *Blindfolding the Muse: The Plight of Painting in the Age of Conceptual Art* (New York: Prenom Press, 1999).

Florence Pennella. "Clarity, Boldness Mark Hyde Park Artist's Work," *Poughkeepsie Journal* (June 17, 1990).

Jed Perl. "Houses, Fields, Gardens, Hills," *The New Criterion* (February 1986).

Vicky Perry. "Catherine Murphy," *artcritical.com* (April 2005).

Peter Plagens. "The Impossible Exhibition," *Newsweek* (April 3, 1995).

_____. "Beauty and Beats," *Newsweek* (September 18, 1995).

Francine Prose. "A Dirty Tablecloth, Deconstructed." *Artnews* (October 1999).

_____. "Catherine Murphy," *Bomb* (Fall 1995).

Carter Ratcliff. "Catherine Murphy at Fourcade, Droll," *Art International* (April 20, 1975).

Vivien Raynor. "The Art of Survival (and Vice Versa)," *The New York Times* (February 17, 1974).

_____. "Art: A Tranquil Show of American Landscapes," *The New York Times* (May 15, 1981).

_____. "Images of New Jersey," *New Jersey Monthly* (November 1981).

_____. "Recent American Still Life," *The New York Times* (November 9, 1984).

Barbara Rose. *American Painting: The Twentieth Century* (New York: Rizzoli, 1986).

_____. "Art as Risky Business," *Vogue* (September 1986).

John Russell. "The Potpourri at Fourcade's," *The New York Times* (February 25, 1977).

_____. "Exchanges II," *The New York Times* (June 20, 1980).

_____. "Art: Show of Drawings at Xavier Fourcade," *The New York Times* (July 29, 1983).

_____. "Catherine Murphy," *The New York Times* (November 29, 1985).

_____. "Catherine Murphy," *The New York Times* (November 11, 1989).

Sanford Schwartz. "New York Letter," *Art International* (May 1973).

Jeanne Silverthorne. "Catherine Murphy," *Artforum* (February 1986).

Roberta Smith. "Mighty Graphitey," *The New York Times* (August 8, 2003).

_____. "Catherine Murphy," *The New York Times* (October 26, 2001).

Deborah Solomon. "All Persuasion, No Whiners: The 1995 Whitney Biennial," *The Wall Street Journal* (March 24, 1995).

_____. "Reality Check," *Vogue* (November 1996).

Gail Stavitsky. "Catherine Murphy," *Arts Magazine* (February 1986).

Mrs. Richard Steele. "Murphy Still Life: Gentle, Detailed and Hard Hitting," *Greensboro Daily News* (October 19, 1975).

Mark Stevens. "Revival of Realism," *Newsweek* (June 7, 1982).

_____. "A Polite Biennial," *New York Magazine* (April 3, 1995).

Patricia Stewart. "Catherine Murphy at Fourcade, Droll," *Art in America* (May-June 1975).

Betsy Sussler, ed. *Speak Art* (New York: New Art Publications/G+B Arts International, 1997).

Robert Taylor. "Painter Catherine Murphy: A Realist with Intelligence," *The Boston Globe* (1976).

Christine Temin. "Art Review: *Boston Collects* a Fascinating Smorgasbord," *The Boston Sunday Globe* (October 26, 1986).

Donna Tennant. "The Americans: The Landscape," *Houston Chronicle* (April 26, 1981).

Marie-France Toinet. "Comment Les États-Unis ont perdu les moyens de leur hégémonie," *Le Monde Diplomatique* (June 1992).

John Wall. "SAMA Show—A Realistic View," *Altoona Mirror* (June 11, 1991).

Mimi Weisbord. "Artists' Choice, Panel Discussion," *Women's Artists Newsletter* (March 1988).

Daniel Wheeler. *Art Since Mid-Century: 1945 to Present* (New York: The Vendome Press, 1991).

Alexi Worth. "Catherine Murphy," *The New Yorker* (October 22, 2001).

John Yau. "Catherine Murphy, Lennon, Weinberg, Inc." *Artforum* (Summer 1992).

_____. "Reality to Infinity: The Drawings of Catherine Murphy," *Art on Paper* (January-February 2001).

_____. "Catherine Murphy in Conversation with John Yau." *The Brooklyn Rail* (February 2005).

_____. "Hedonist of the Ordinary," in *Catherine Murphy: New Work* (Knoedler & Company, 2008).

William Zimmer. "At the Neuberger, Windows Allow Artists to Share a Theme," *The New York Times* (October 12, 1986).

PUBLIC COLLECTIONS

Achenbach Foundation for Graphic Arts, California Palace of the Legion of Honor, San Francisco

The Art Institute of Chicago

Boise Art Museum

Canton Museum of Art

Chase Manhattan Bank, New York

Cranbrook Art Museum, Bloomfield Hills

Frye Art Museum, Seattle

Georgia Museum of Art, The University of Georgia, Athens

Greenville County Museum of Art, Greenville

Hirshhorn Museum and Sculpture Garden, Washington, DC

The Frances Lehman Loeb Art Center, Vassar College, Poughkeepsie

The Metropolitan Museum of Art, New York

Museum of Fine Arts, Boston

The Museum of Modern Art, New York

The Newark Museum

New Jersey State Museum, Trenton

New York Public Library, Astor, Lenox, and Tilden Foundation, New York

The Phillips Collection, Washington, DC

Smithsonian American Art Museum, Washington, DC

The University of Michigan Museum of Art, Ann Arbor

Virginia Museum of Fine Arts, Richmond

Weatherspoon Art Museum, University of North Carolina at Greensboro

Whitney Museum of American Art, New York

Published on the occasion of the exhibition
Catherine Murphy
New Work
May 1–August 1, 2008

Knoedler & Company
19 East 70 Street, New York, New York 10021
Tel 212 794-0550 Fax 212 772-6932
www.knoedlergallery.com

Cover: *Hand Mirror*, 2008, oil on canvas, 46 x 54 1/2 inches (detail)
Frontispiece: *Nuts and Shells*, 2005, graphite on paper, 29 1/2 x 37 inches

Color transparencies by Jeff Sturges, New York and On Location,
Poughkeepsie, New York
Catalogue designed by The Grenfell Press, New York
Printed by Trifolio, Verona, Italy
Essay copyright © 2008 John Yau
Images copyright © 2008 Catherine Murphy
Publication copyright © 2008 Knoedler & Company
All rights reserved

Published in an edition of 3000

ISBN: 0-9789987-8-2